Emergence

Emergence

A WOMAN'S LIFE THROUGH
POETRY AND MOTION

BY
SUSAN CAMBIGUE TRACEY

WITH
PAUL TRACEY

Emergence: A Woman's Life Through Poetry and Motion
by Susan Cambigue Tracey
with Paul Tracey

© Copyright Susan Cambigue Tracey

ISBN 978-1-7348787-3-8 (trade paperback original)
First edition published December 2021

Many of the poems included in *Emergence* originated in sessions of ShiftPoetry™, a program developed and run by Howard Kern and Barbara Ligeti.

All rights reserved. No part of this book may be reproduced in any form or by any electronic or mechanical means, including information storage and retrieval systems, without permission in writing from the publisher, except by a reviewer, who may quote brief passages in a review. For permissions, please write to address below or email barbaraligeti@mac.com. Any members of education institutions wishing to photocopy or electronically reproduce part or all of the work for classroom use, or publishers who would like to obtain permission to include the work in an anthology, should send their inquiries to ShiftPoetry™ c/o Barbara Ligeti, 910 West End Avenue—Suite 6F, New York, NY 10025.

COVER AND BOOK DESIGN:
KG Design International
www.katgeorges.com
kgeokat@mac.com

ShiftPoetry Press
910 West End Avenue Suite 6F
New York, New York 10025
www.ShiftPoetry.com

DEDICATION

I dedicate this book to my daughter, Julianne Bennett Cambigue, and to all mothers and fathers who have lost a child to an untimely death.

The great Kahlil Gibran, poet and philosopher, wrote in The Prophet, *"You are the bows from which your children as living arrows are sent forth . . ."*

As a parent I expected Julie to travel into the future to fulfill her dreams. With her death, my hopes were shattered. The one thing that sustains me is that I believe her spirit still exists—and I know our time together was not wasted.

TABLE OF CONTENTS

FOREWORD i

PREFACE *My Life is a Candle* v

INTRODUCTION vii

PART I: THE EGG AND THE LARVA 1
Rolling Down Grassy Knolls 2
Jerry Gonzales—My Very First Best Friend 4
The Rag Doll 7
Reading To Find Meaning 8
Locked Up 10
She Is My Mother—But Not My Best Friend 12
My Last Meal 16
Getting My Way! 18
My Wise Guide 20
Summers Past 23

PART II: FROM LARVA TO CATERPILLAR 27
A Perfect Birthday! 28
Pets—A Source of Joy? 29
Trapeze Artist: A How-To Guide 32
Porgy and Bess 34
A Return to the Ice 36
Near, Yet Apart and Lonely 39
Death of a Princess 41
Telling My Parents 44
The State of Abundance 46
A Graduation to Honor 50
An Empty Life 52

CONTENTS *(continued)*

PART III: BUILDING A COCOON 55
A Walk on the Beach in African Hats —
    A Different Kind of Intimacy 56
A Honeymoon in Scotland 61
Combining Groups. 62
The Tuileries Gardens—Paris 63
My Deepest Loss. 64
Julianne 65
Off With My Breast!. 66
My Attitude Now 68
First Save Yourself. 69

PART IV: A BUTTERFLY EMERGES & TAKES FLIGHT 73
Red-Tailed Hawk—Freedom Through Perspective 74
No Funny Bone. 76
What Can I Change—What Can I Not? 78
Give, Take, Hold Onto—Or Let Go. 81
An Archeological Dig Through Photos 83
A Rite of Passage for Skylar. 86
A Virtual Bucket List. 90
Passages—Rites Or Rights?. 92
The Movie Version of My Life 94

CONTENTS *(continued)*

PART V: FREE FLIGHT—SOARING	99
An Ideal Relationship	100
Joy in Bed	102
Channel a Tree	103
If I Could Choose—I Would Want a Gardener	105
My Covid Bubble	108
A Fairy Tale That Needs a Happy Ending	110
Alone Time—Too Much?	113
Empty Spaces, Turtles and Time	117
The Greatest Gift of All	120
There . . . Go I	121
A Trip to the Unseen	122
EPILOGUE: A VIEW FROM THE ROOF	127
BIOS	129
Susan Cambigue Tracey's Bio	129
Paul Tracey's Bio, in his own voice	131
ACKNOWLEDGMENTS	133
INDEX OF PHOTOGRAPHS	134

FOREWORD

Susan Cambigue Tracey and I met in 2017, when I signed up for yoga as a means of exercising and quieting my "monkey brain" as I recovered from a hamstring injury. About a year earlier, I had been diagnosed for the second time with prostate cancer. Following the first diagnosis back in 2013, I opted for surgery to remove my prostate. Though the doctors were skeptical that this would work, I was hopeful. I was right for three years until I was wrong.

With the second diagnosis, the only medical option was to take hormone blockers to stop the production of testosterone, which doctors believe feeds the cancer. My family wanted me to do as the doctors directed. I was tired of following orders. My decision led to great unrest within my family and ultimately contributed to the end of my marriage.

Susan helped me to deal with my personal challenges. She was not only my yoga teacher but also my mentor and friend. From the moment I limped into that yoga studio, I felt both secure and strong in her presence. She and I developed a special relationship.

At the time we met, poetry was my way of accepting and sharing my feelings. Not everyone got my poetry, but Susan did. I also learned how to write in the voices of other people. Susan was one of my favorite models and I wrote many poems that were inspired by her.

Like many people, she'd had her share of tragedy, including divorce, losing a child, breast cancer, and just normal life events. However, she weathered these experiences and used them as inspiration to serve others and live a life full of gratitude and not despair.

Part of my attraction to Susan was that she was the same age as my mother would have been had she not unfortunately passed away four years earlier. My mother had been a loving woman but was limited by traditional values. Susan was both loving and open-minded. She was wide-eyed and accepting. I was able to communicate my fears and concerns to her without feeling judged. She also shared her life experiences with me.

After yoga class, we would go across the street to Starbucks and sit at a table and talk about current events and I would read my poetry to her. After about a year, Susan told me that she too enjoyed writing poetry.

Susan exposed me to many valuable lessons based on her own experiences and that of others. She taught me how to age gracefully. She shared a book with me titled, "The Yamas and Niyamas – The Ten Principles for Peace and Purpose," by Deborah Adele, which taught me how to let go of things, even relationships, which had become more harmful than productive. She also helped me to gain balance in my life, first through yoga and then through breathing. But the most important lesson I learned from her was to do everything with a loving heart and let go of anger, which serves no purpose.

Subsequent to meeting Susan, I met Barbara Ligeti, who co-created the technology we call ShiftPoetry™. Barbara and I started ShiftPoetry™ in 2018 as workshops to help people access their emotions via writing poetry. During a typical workshop, detailed prompts are read; people are given ten minutes to write "poetically and from the heart." They write whatever comes to mind, and then read their poems to the group. Susan, being a close friend and supporter, attended these workshops. Happily, they inspired her to pursue her writing openly and voraciously. ShiftPoetry™ ultimately motivated Susan to share her full and luscious life in this book.

I have been lucky to have heard Susan's stories in person. However, I did not want to be selfish and I urged her to reach a wider forum. Reading this book, the words that come to mind are "elegance" and "grace." Whether it is the darkest moments or the lightest, Susan shares her life honestly and openly, and provides a roadmap so that others can also face adversity courageously and come out better versions of themselves.

I am proud that I contributed to her inspiration, but the words and the experiences are all Susan's.

HOWARD KERN
Attorney, Author and
Co-Founder of ShiftPoetry™

PREFACE

My Life is a Candle

We are only here
for a candle's worth of time
Burning brightly -
a tear, a drop of rain, an exhale
can blow us out
Nothingness . . .
smoke signals our exit
spiraling upward -
our spirit disappears.
Thick, white wax
melted
lies motionless.

INTRODUCTION

This is my life story, realized and recorded in my poems. I began writing at age 14, inspired by my high school English teacher who guided her students in exploring our own observations, stories and emotional struggles through poetry. I was hooked! I began writing at home just for fun. It became one of my life passions. My poems in this book will reveal a great deal, but I will give you a little taste of who I am in this introduction.

I grew up in Southern California in a very traditional family of four people—mother, father, younger brother and me. My parents came from modest backgrounds and, with intentional purpose and hard work, built an extraordinary life for all of us. From the time I was three or four, I frequently asked my parents, "Why am I here? What am I supposed to do?" I felt as if I had come into this life with a mission—though I didn't yet know what it was. They told me I was supposed to explore my little world—be curious, learn and play. The rest would be revealed over time. I accepted that explanation, allowing it to satisfy me, yet today I am still looking forward to what comes next—each day, each year, and each lifetime.

You see, I believe in multiple lifetimes. Regardless, I still accept that the only world I know for certain is this one I'm living in right now. In it, I have experienced both great joy and devastating sorrow.

There is a story about a man who had a vision. He was walking along a beach with God. Scenes of his life flashed before him in which he saw two sets of footprints on the sand. But at the worst points in his life, he only saw one set.

The man asked, "How come during the hardest times of my life there is only one set of footprints? Why did you abandon me?"

God answered, "I did not abandon you. I carried you."

For me, much of my life has unfolded smoothly. Sometimes I had no questions. At other times, the only way I made it through was to trust in a higher power to guide me. Remarkably, specific people came into my life at the right times to assist. I felt I was being led, and sometimes carried.

Everyone has a story. Mine has come to me in poetry; sometimes in rhythmic patter, and other times in prose-like phrases. In writing poems, my thoughts have been clarified.

This book is a compilation of stories drawn from my life, expressed through my poetry. No doubt you will arrive at your own impressions of me and my story; we may agree, maybe not. The beauty of poetry is that all points of view are valid and valued. Hopefully this work will inspire you to mine your own experiences and write about them.

I haven't revealed some parts of my life with other people until now. In this book I lift the shades so that others can witness my experiences and my philosophy of life.

Like a butterfly, we start out as a tiny egg that hatches into a caterpillar, which then builds a sheltering cocoon around itself, morphs into a pupa in its chrysalis before emerging as a beautiful and transcendent butterfly. It is a full transformation, just as all of our lives are.

For me, life is a continuum—I have always had visions of past lives—some, in worlds other than Earth. As I grow closer to the end of this latest life, I feel quite certain that it is a culmination of what I have experienced since my beginning. After my last breath, I expect this trajectory will resume in future incarnations—here or elsewhere.

From the transcendent butterfly phase of my life I reflect back with love and understanding on my emergence. My hope is that my words will guide other people to savor every phase of life through to the last.

SUSAN CAMBIGUE TRACEY
Pacific Palisades, CA
October 20, 2021

Emergence

Part I

THE EGG & THE LARVA

Through the Eyes of a Young Girl

ROLLING DOWN GRASSY KNOLLS

Rolling down grassy knolls,
    over and over again!
Climbing back up,
    skin itching,
        I lie down and roll over and over again -
        until I am dizzy and disoriented,
        trying to stand,
        finally falling onto the grass
        at the bottom of the hill.

Laying on my back
    I look up into the sky,
    clouds capturing my interest
    with their changing shapes -
Pigs and Elephants,
    Boats and Trains.

WAIT!

A flock of sheep are eating
    their way across the sky!

I could lie here for hours in the middle of Spring
    feeling happy and dizzy -
A part of the world,
    changing as I lie still in the grass!

Rolling over, I search for lady bugs,
    tiny, yellow flowers and ...
    especially for four-leaf clovers.

Time is an experience rather than a measurement.

I feel happy,
> connected to the wind,
> the earth and the trees.

I am especially happy to be free,
> being part of the day,
> watching it change.

JERRY GONZALES — MY VERY FIRST BEST FRIEND

Until I was five
    we lived on East Fifth Street
    in Los Angeles,
    East of downtown,
    near an Episcopal Church
    I attended - and
    Rowen Ave. Elementary School -
    the first school my father and I
    both attended 40 years apart.

It was a real neighborhood,
    houses lined up side by side,
    each with a fireplace, front and back yard.
Children of all ages played
    Hide and Seek together -
    calling out, "Ollie Ollie Oxen
    Free - Free - Free!"
    when we safely touched the tall palm tree -
    Home Base.

I was one of the youngest.
Jerry Gonzales, also my age,
    was my best friend.
We didn't really know
    the rules - so we hid together
    giggling - then screaming
    when we were easily found!

He lived four houses from me.
We played together every day.
Our favorite thing was swinging.
Two homemade swings hung
    from ropes looped around the
    strong branches of our Pepper Tree.

He had a swing in his yard too.
Sometimes I was invited to
    Sunday dinner with his family.
I really liked Jerry and
    he liked me!

One Sunday morning
    I went to play with him.
We sat together on a wide,
    wooden swing seat,
    each holding onto the side ropes.
Swinging happily back and forth,
    we sang songs and laughed.

His grandmother opened
    the kitchen door,
    and walked into the yard.
We waved to her. She waved back.

Then, she grabbed one of their
    free-range chickens by the neck,
    placed it on a stump
    in front of us - and
    chopped its head off!
My mouth opened wide!

I can still see the headless body
    frantically running around.
I was horrified, yet fascinated
    at this feat! Only later
    did I make the connection -
    it was that chicken which provided dinner.

I cherish my first friendship
    with Jerry Gonzales!

THE RAG DOLL

Little dolly sitting there,
Made of rags and red yarn hair.
Do you long to laugh and run?
Instead of watching all the fun?

Little dolly standing there,
Propped against the baby's chair.
If the wind could make you real,
Would you enjoy the way you feel?

Little dolly lying there,
Soiled and torn by years of wear.
Children shared their thoughts with you,
Laughed and cried, and loved you too.

Though you can't laugh and run yourself,
You should sit proudly on the shelf -
For you have served a purpose rare,
By teaching little ones to care.

READING TO FIND MEANING

When I was in first grade
    I was placed in the Yellow Reading Group.
My friends were in the Green Group.
Why were we not together?
I was with the poor readers.
Why?
I was surprised at their struggles.
I glanced over at my friends.
They were taking turns
    reading to each other.
In my group,
    children were having difficulty identifying letter sounds!
I was shocked!

Why was I in this group?
The teacher was patient,
    helping each child.
Finally, she asked me to read -
    I did.
She seemed surprised, but relieved.
Now I understood.
I was in this group as her helper.
I felt proud,
    needed,
        appreciated.
I was happy!

A week later
    I was placed in the Green Group with my friends.
Later still,
    I learned I had not initially tested well.
Placed in the Yellow Group
    I could have lost confidence.
Actually, I found my calling -
    BE A TEACHER!

LOCKED UP

My dad was a Judge.
I sat in his court from an early age,
    watching people play their roles -
Court Reporter, Clerk, Lawyers,
    Witnesses, Victims, Defendants - those accused of crimes.

But,
    the one I was most afraid of was the bailiff.
He had a gun in a holster slung from his waist.
He also had handcuffs,
    which I saw him lock onto the wrists of prisoners.
This was the one person
    I didn't want to cross.
I liked my freedom.
I could feel the pain of those restrained.

On a long chain attached to his belt
    there was a key
    to release the cuffs.
I watched the bailiff very carefully
    never wanting to catch his attention.
I slid down in my seat
    trying to be invisible
    if he looked up.
I could feel the pain of losing my freedom.

Then,
    one night the bailiff came to dinner!
I was horrified -
    thinking he would take me to jail.
My father asked him to show me the handcuffs.
I viscerally withdrew, my eyes wide.

He asked if I wanted to try them on.
I stood frozen in fear.
He asked me to hold out both my hands.
Then,
    he enclosed my wrists in the heavy silver rings.
I was unable to move!
I couldn't breathe!
I was his prisoner -
    compliant, defeated, scared, worried.
I would never be free again.

I knew then I would never disobey the law.
Prison was not for me.
I knew then -
    I will always obey the law.

SHE IS MY MOTHER - BUT NOT MY BEST FRIEND

It is not just one conversation -
    but a series of talks
    that I wish I could have with my mother.
My mother was kind, wise, deeply fair and honest.
She advised me and always spoke truth -
Things I needed to know,
    things I needed to change.
I always knew she loved me with all her being.

As a child of four,
    I told her she was my best friend.
It was a shock when she said that she was my mother
    and she couldn't be my best friend.

Shocked and saddened,
    I felt the space between us grow.
She was not me;
    I was not her.

Even then,
    I knew she was my guide.
We could not share things that people the same age do.
I wanted to be like her.
I wanted to be wrapped in her kind smile and admiration.

I didn't want her separateness.
By her words,
    she separated herself from me.
She pushed me out into the bigger world.
I had to earn my friendships.
Love would come from others
    only when they saw me as separate.

Realizing I was alone,
    I observed the world to see how others fit in.
I copied my mother's gracefulness,
    I admired her wit - sharp and intelligent.
That was something I couldn't match.
I saw her interest in others,
    her playfulness,
    her ability to be an equal partner to my father,
BUT -
    recognizing him as the King of our Family
AND -
    it must be said that he treated her as his Queen.
My brother and I were the next generation of equals.

Years passed.
My mother slid back into a return of breast cancer,
    metastasizing into her organs,
        I gave her the best support I could.
She was strong, uncomplaining,
    and still in her role as my mother,
    protecting me,
    modeling acceptance, strength, courage -
    even hope.

She wanted me,
    needed me,
    but wouldn't come down to my level.
She wanted my friendship,
    but couldn't accept us as equals.
She was still my mother,
    I was still her daughter.
She still had more to teach me.

During this time of death and dying,
    she shared her fears with my father,
    but only her strength with me.

I wish I could have been my mother's friend.
I wish I could have been the strong one for her.
I wish I could have carried her burden,
    but it was clear from the beginning.
She was my mother, my teacher, my friend
    but not my Best Friend.
She knew that I needed to form bonds with people,
    those who would remain my companions
    when she was gone.

As a grown woman,
    I grasp what she gave me.
What she taught me as my mother,
    outlasts friendship.
It is of greater purpose.
She knew her job was to teach me all life's skills,
    with compassion.
I would need to solve my own problems,
    negotiate my own relationships
    and make plans for my life's journey.

It is true!
She was my mother, my guide, my model.
I have an independence borne of her belief in my ability,
    sustainability, courage and wisdom.
Martha Emily Rannells Bennett -
    my mother, my guide, my friend -
    but, not my best friend!

MY LAST MEAL

My Last Meal?
It isn't even a contest!
I've traveled to many countries,
    different cultures - but
    my favorite meal is the one
    I grew up with - Mexican food!

Especially Mexican food made by
    my Anglo-Saxon American mother.
We lived in a neighborhood with
    many Hispanic people.
The standard was tacos, enchiladas,
    refried beans, chile rellenos -
And, of course, chips, guacamole and salsa!

My taste buds were set early.
Even my tall, white grandfather,
    most days,
    ate chile con carne for lunch.

Then, my father discovered
    El Cholo Spanish Restaurant
    on Western in Hollywood.
It was the gourmet version of
    Mexican food I grew up on.
We became regulars!
I grew to love chips and medium salsa -
    later, Margaritas and
    Corona beer with lime slices.

My mother grew interested in
    creating this food from scratch -
    buying raw pinto beans -
    boiling them for hours and then
    smashing them and making
    refried beans - yum!
Spanish rice came next -
    with fresh fried tomatoes.

She created our favorite
    home-styled Mexican dinner -
    four crispy tacos apiece.
Two filled with
    refried beans and melted cheese.
Two filled with
    finely separated ground beef and onions,
    bowls of other ingredients
    to add - if we wished -
    lettuce, spicy salsa,
    black olives and sour cream - Yum!

Add both a Margarita and a beer -
    it becomes my Last Meal.

GETTING MY WAY!

Saturday!
Movies - Friends -
Freedom from structure, freedom from chores.
My parents were rooted in their beautiful garden.
Saturdays were a time for them to assist
    the miracles of growing things.
Weed. Dig. Clip. Rake. Gather. Haul.

"Susan, will you help?"
Anger arises within me
    being asked - expected - to help.
Resistance turns to anger.
Anger turns to tacit agreement to join this effort.

Bugs! Bees! Spiders! Worms!
Garden snakes lay hidden between the leaves -
    even underground.
Also, flying, crawling, diving bugs.
Insects that sting my legs and arms.
I move slowly, not understanding their instructions -
    making them repeat them.

Carrying leaves in a canvas bag,
    I drop them,
    scattering them as dried confetti,
    causing confusion - causing frustration.
I take their pleasure out of gardening.
I complain and drag my feet heavily
    through each task I am given.

I see the beauty of this well-loved garden,
    I feel their joy as they work in harmony,
I am discord.
I am destructive.
I am cruel.

I want to go to the movies!

Finally
    I deeply scratch myself on the bark of a tree.
My mother leaves her work to tend to me.

Finally, I get what I want.
My father's bass voice bellows out,

"Susan - do us a big favor and leave!
Go to the movies.
Just leave us in peace.
We love our garden.
You can pick flowers later,
    make pretty bouquets for the table.
Read a book in the crook of a tree,
    but leave the work of the garden to us.
Working in the garden is a joy,
    not a punishment."

MY WISE GUIDE

Mambo -
    my maternal grandmother,
    soft skin, round frame, sparkling eyes -
    kindness spilling over the edges of her heart.
We lived a day's car ride away
    so I only saw her once a year.
But we had a deep connection -
    from the beginning to the end.

She listened to me,
> believed in my dreams.

She was psychic and communed with spirits
> in the world without bodies.

I had similar experiences
> but no one believed me - except her.

She had no one to share with -
> so we had secret conversations
> about life and death -
> and the world beyond.

When I was little,
> I would lay my head in her lap.

She would run her fingers through my hair
> and lovingly rub my back.

Adult conversations between those in the room
> flowed in and out of my consciousness.

I felt safe.
I felt loved.
I felt accepted for being me.

She had planned her next life.
This time 'round she was
> a wife, mother and grandmother.

Next, she planned to be a professional woman.
I admired her for that.

She grew up in a mining town.
Everyone was poor -
> all at the mercy of the mine owners
> who ran the local store.

She married her true love at 18.

They had met at a dance when she was 17.
She asked him when he might marry.
He said, "On the day you do!"
He was also a miner - and lost an eye -
   in the quicksilver mines.

Mambo birthed six children,
     reaped 16 grandchildren,
     and multiple great grandchildren.
In her 80s she saw new possibilities.
She fulfilled her current responsibilities first.
She was almost done.
Mambo was one of my role models -
     inspiring me to be
     true to myself,
     and the commitments I make.

SUMMERS PAST

Summer has always been
    a time out.
Days seem longer.

Fun oozes out of my
    daydreams.
Summers at the beach
    lying in the warm sun,
    the sound of ocean waves crashing,
    lapping on the shore.
Wading in the surf,
    I see bubbles in the wet sand -
    the secret life of sand crabs -
    hidden from my view.
Seagulls squawking,
    trying to steal my lunch.
I sit looking out over the dark,
    blue-green seascape imagining
    other lands beyond my sight.

Clouds form - creating a series of skyscapes,
    ever changing tableaux,
    given meaning by my imagination.
Summer is a time for thoughts to run free.
Looking across the water,
    I imagine other lives,
    new possibilities,
    contemplating my future
    under my large straw hat.
I see my past,
    my present,
    and think of summers of my youth.
That was the time when
    summer had the most meaning.
The greatest contrast
    with my responsible life.
Summers are a time for dreaming,
    a time for relaxing,
    collecting seashells and rocks,
    standing ankle deep in the water,
    feeling the tide try to pull me off balance -
    out to sea.

Part II
From LARVA to CATERPILLAR
A Young Woman Explores & Grows

A PERFECT BIRTHDAY!

Confetti!
Sprinkles of color
Blue sky with warm sunlight
Laughter
Spanish guitars playing
Music carried by the breeze
I dance along the path to New Adventures,
Green Corn Tamales in February,
Not just April through October!
I bestow wishes upon everyone!
Wishes come true!
Believe in each person
Joy in each wish,
Some wish for more.
Wish wisely
Responsibly
Evolve
Gift the world
Transform human character -
Start with yourself!
Goodness, Righteousness,
Justice for all.
Above all,
Loving Kindness and Truth
Wish to deepen your soul
Connect with others
Wish to be free -
Be your best self!
Manifest your dreams.
Happy Birthday to all!

PETS - A SOURCE OF JOY?

Pets are not currently
    an intimate part
    of my life - however,
    much of my life was filled with
    dogs, cats, ducks, birds, a lamb,
    a rabbit and 4 tame rats!

The most lovely to look at
    were our four large, white ducks -
    Daisy, Donald, Kiqui and Quack-Quack,
    each with a four-foot wing span.
Although their wings were clipped,
    they did manage to fly onto
    the lower limbs of our apricot tree
    when a barking dog broke into our yard!

From time to time
      we would eat some of the eggs
      that Daisy laid.
None became little ducklings,
      and the taste of
      her eggs was quite strong.

While it was awe-inspiring to
      see them from our bathroom window
      as we brushed our teeth,
      it could be messy
      to walk across our yard,
      slipping and sliding precariously.
Our ducks were indiscriminate in
      dropping their waste -
The entire grass was a
"WATCH YOUR STEP!" zone.

A large children's pool
      was filled for their pleasure -
      but as soon as I cleaned it,
      they busily worked to
      carry dirt in their bills,
      dropping it into the water.
They were not worried about
      pooping there either.

They held us hostage in our house.
It was not pleasant to be in our yard.
Our gardener threatened to quit!
I didn't know what to do.

Months passed . . .
Then, one Saturday my father came -
    unannounced -
    to rescue us.
He lifted four crates from his car.
Putting one duck in each,
    he assured me
    he was taking them to
    Lincoln Park Lake - in East L.A . . . .
Many ducks resided there.

I didn't resist.
I was too tired - and relieved.
He drove off -
    with our four ducks quacking.
Relief washed over me.
I emptied the pool.
I hosed down the grass.
I fixed us lunch - which we ate in our yard.

The next day he came again.
Two cages - each with a small parakeet inside.
    Green for Julie - blue for Heather

TRAPEZE ARTIST
A HOW-TO GUIDE

Trapeze artists,
    defining trust,
    taking risks
    knowing they will be caught.

Swinging, flying, holding on, letting go.
Secure - Responsible - Daring - Free
    within limits.
Flung through space
    caught in flight - mid-air.
Released from
    Doubts - Fear - Distrust - Resistance.
Bones lighter than air!
Trust stronger than steel.
Timing is everything!
Some are catchers - Some are flyers.
Each plays their part.
All are needed.
No slippery fingers
    among this group.

We all can learn from this troupe.
Relationships only work
    with trust and support,
    momentum and flight,
    safe landings and unity.
Strong beginnings - clean endings -
    the middle is risk and adventure.
Everyone in a family has a role.
Each must be valued,
    trusted,
    alert to each other's needs,
    knowing when to support,
    when to let someone fly free.
Balance and instincts govern,
    and…
    when one falls -
    catch them in a net of unconditional love!

PORGY AND BESS

Various pets have been companions throughout my life -
    mainly dogs and cats,
        but also rabbits, parakeets, rats and fish,
        as well as a small, beloved turtle.

However,
    my favorites were two black cats.
The male was Porgy,
    the female was Bess.
Bess was timid and shy -
    hesitant around people.
Porgy was bold, brave,
    and devoted to my daughter, Julie.

Porgy followed Julie like a dog.
Played with her,
    and cuddled up against her small body at night.
She made costumes for him,
    which he tolerated.
He played supportive roles in her plays.
He was loyal and devoted -
    as much as a cat can be.
She felt safe.

When she was seven,
    she wanted to sleep in a tent
    pitched in our back yard
    right outside our bedroom windows.
After days of pleading,
    we let her do it -
    knowing Porgy would be with her,
    comforting her - protecting her.

She felt safe as long as Porgy was with her.
We were still nervous,
    and kept alert all night.
She fell asleep quickly -
    independent and a bit wild,
        certainly stubborn and willful.

Porgy seemed to understand her -
    he never left her side.

A RETURN TO THE ICE

I just love ice-skating.
Blue Jay, near Lake Arrowhead,
    had an outdoor rink.
Many talented skaters put on demonstrations.
Sometimes, anyone could skate.
From a young age,
    my family would spend weekends in Lake Arrowhead.

We would stay in a cabin
    nestled in the forest,
        tall trees surrounded us.
My grandfather snored loudly at night.
It was very cold. Brrr…
In the evenings,
    we had an impressive fire in a stone hearth.
That was fun.
The comfort of family
    made me feel like I belonged.
Paper napkins were filled with fresh popcorn.
It was dark -
    few electric lights and candles.
But it was an adventure!

I waited for the days to begin -
    for light to appear,
        shyly creeping through the dense branches.
A large breakfast eaten together - yummy!
Pancakes, bacon and eggs,
    the fragrant aroma of brewed coffee.

Dressed warmly,
    we ventured outside for hikes,
    building snow people,
    chasing squirrels.
Deer quietly nibbled at morsels on the forest floor.

Then,
    a car trip to the nearby villages.
My favorite was Blue Jay and the ice rink.
Outdoors with a covered roof,
    we could watch lessons,
    rehearsals,
    and sometimes a show.

On special occasions,
    we rented skates,
    tentatively making our way around the edge,
    holding onto the sides of the rink
    or clinging to each other -
    preferably to my mother,
    the best in our family of untrained skaters,
    and the one I had access to.

As we struggled to stay upright,
    we all got better.
I even learned to do cross-overs
    around the curves
    and skate backwards,
    slowly.
I loved the flow and grace of the professionals.
I channeled skaters in the performances.
Even some students learned to spin and leap.
I never got the chance to work with a teacher.

Instead,
> I cloned Sonja Henie,
> an Olympic champion I watched
> on newsreels and films!

Years later,
> I took my daughters ice skating.

I didn't have the funds to give them lessons.
They struggled just as I had.
Taking breaks for hot chocolate
> and melted marshmallows -
> sometimes a burger!

In my mind,
> I continue to ice-skate,
> feeling the confidence, grace and joy of Sonja Henie.

Chair Yoga flow poses lend themselves to
> the arm and leg movements of skaters.

This is fulfilling to me now.

However,
> one never knows -
> I might decide to take lessons.

If I do, it will be to perform
> a duet on ice -
> I hope he is a professional partner!

NEAR, YET APART AND LONELY

One fish in a glass bowl
    seeing the world outside,
    but never engaged.
Swimming round and round,
    her world is comforting, but boring.
Called Goldie, she never hears her name.

Big eyes pressed to the slick curve of her bowl,
    lips moving - but no sounds.
She sees moving shapes and colors.
She is lonely
    but doesn't know it.

One day another fish appears
    in her bowl,
    in a plastic bag,
    placed in her world,
    but with no contact.
Two fish in the same bowl, but in separate worlds.
No ability to rub fins,
    or blow bubbles together,
    no games of chase or follow the leader.
Two fish spirits - kept apart.
Transparent walls - no contact.
Would one eat the other?
Be curious?
Would they become friends?
Lovers?
Fight for control of their water world?

Alas, no communication -
- two separate fish souls -
- space divided - yet transparent - with borders
- sharing one bowl; divided by a plastic bag -
- into two worlds.

Separate,
- swimming around each other -
- never together in the same space.

If things were different,
Would they be friends?
Does the other fish even have a name?

DEATH OF A PRINCESS

When I was a child
I watched in delight
Clouds in the day
Bright stars at night

There was hope in the sky
And change could I see
Rainbows and Heaven
Were versions of me

I spoke to the wind
Shaping thoughts in the air
Blowing into the future
My life - with great care

I was a princess
I was a bride
I was a mother
Babies waiting inside

Life was so good
Time didn't matter
Spaces to dream in
And fill up with chatter

I sprang from the rainbows
And danced on the clouds
Never knowing that some day
They'd serve as my shroud

The princess, one day
Fell out of her dreams
Tumbled and shattered
She cried silent screams

She thought she could fly
She thought she had wings
But on her first flight
There were transparent strings

Strings were attached to
"Accepting" the part
of the princess and bride -
Right from the start

Story book angels
Daughters and brides
Never leave the safe cover
Of the stories inside

Now I'm a woman
I've grown through the years
The pain and the loss
Have mellowed my tears

The fairy tale's shattered
The princess is dead
But I am alive
And go forth instead

TELLING MY PARENTS...

I never thought
    I would be a divorced woman.
I never thought
    I would be a single mom.
When I went with my husband, Lee,
  to tell my parents the news,
  they said two things -

    "You have ruined the lives of your children, forever."

And
    "You are the first person in our family to get divorced.
      You have brought shame upon all of us!"

As shocking as these words sound,
    I knew that they were actually
    born out of deep anguish,
      rather than meanness.
I knew how much my parents loved us all.
This was a big shock to them.
They told me -

    "You have made your bed.
    You must now sleep in it!
    You can't move back in with us!"

I was on my own.
I had to figure out a way
    to redesign my life.
They set boundaries that
    kept me strong -
      and highly motivated.

It was very lonely.
I realized that even being
    married and together,
    one can feel isolated when
    the other emotionally draws away.
Maybe I was the one withdrawing -
    I just knew I was stuck
    in a life that was
    not making me happy.
It was complex -
    it always is -
    because so many other people are
    impacted by this decision.

I felt isolated wherever I went.
Even though I had very little income,
    I had a cleaning woman
    once a month and
    I got mini massages.
At that time, I was teaching
    fifteen classes a week in different places.
Getting me and the kids ready each morning
    was a major event.

But, I felt free!

THE STATE OF ABUNDANCE

I grew up with parents who had
    both grown up poor.
Their families struggled
    to have enough.
They were each determined to
    change their status in life -
    through education and hard work.
Each one worked while paying for
    a university education.
That's where they met - Berkeley -
    each on the edge of a dream,
    full of hope.
They remained thrifty as a couple,
    living with my father's parents.

Then, they had a child (me)
    and put a down payment on a small home
    in East Los Angeles.
My father was a lawyer; my mother his secretary.
My father cut out every coupon
    from several papers
    every day.
His shopping trips
    included a series of stores
    with sales on specific products and food.
No one-stop shopping for him.
His ritual was performed
    on Saturday mornings.

When he returned,
    it was like a celebration.
He sat us down at the kitchen table.
Unpacking, we learned of all he purchased.
Handing out toothpaste, combs,
    Cracker Jacks, peanuts in their shells -
    with a flourish.
He was proud to provide for us.
He made shopping for necessities
    seem like a birthday party.
He was so excited by
    all his purchases -
    made possible with coupons -
    many times getting two for the price of one.

So, I never felt poor -
    and we weren't poor.
By the time I arrived
    their status had changed.
But, not their attitude.
I always felt an atmosphere of abundance -
    there was enough.
An emotion of enthusiasm prevailed.
Buying something often required patience -
    patience was always rewarded.

After I was divorced,
> I needed a new car.

I discussed it with my parents.
They encouraged me to
> research what it would cost,
> then, figure out a way
> to save the money.

It took me two years to add onto
> my savings of $5,000.

I needed $10,000 to buy the car I wanted -
> a bright red Ford Mustang!

I was coming to have dinner
> with my parents -
> they had been babysitting
> my two daughters.

I waited until dessert, then announced
> I saved the money - $10,000.

I can buy a new car!

My parents were silent.
They looked at each other.
Then,
> my father looked me in the eyes.

He paused and said,

"Now that you have saved the money,
 we would like to buy you that car!"

I was shocked - even hurt.

"What? You would take away
 the reward I worked for?"

Our words tangled, then split apart.
I was hurt; they were adamant!
They were buying me a car.
I could pick it out -
 with my father!

A GRADUATION TO HONOR

No graduations loom in my near future.
I only have memories of ones in the past.
For me, it is a time of relief, accomplishment,
    and taking steps to create a new chapter in my life.
That's the way it was for me when I graduated from UCLA.

Two weeks later, I was married,
    giving myself no time or opportunities to experience
    life on my own.
No longer a student,
    I was a fledging adult.
So, I married a man who appeared to be a full adult.
A man in a suit, who had a job and a car.
Together, we bought a small house.
We both went off to work after our summer honeymoon.
I shopped, cooked, cleaned house,
    and gave dinner parties for his work colleagues.
We had two children.
I was living the life I had envisioned during my college years -
    but it wasn't fulfilling.
Something was missing.
I didn't know what.
I just felt lonely in my togetherness.
I felt empty in my filling up with family life.
I kept thinking, is this all there is?
What more was I longing for?

So, for 15 years I continued along the path
    I had taken after graduation.
I just kept going on the same trajectory -
    moving, but without that inner spark of excitement,
    I felt trapped.
We finally released each other to go our separate ways.
In that time I grew up and found myself.
Who was I?
What did I need to be more of?
The true graduation of my life was to be married -
    so I was forced to grow -
    to break the expectations I had for the perfect life.

What resembled disaster -
    led me to find the perfect life -
    I have finally graduated from innocence to
    living an adult life.

AN EMPTY LIFE

My anxiety -
    being in an empty life.
Empty thoughts.
Empty reasons for living.
Being here - alone with myself.
Fear that the future is unfilled,
    sitting on the sidelines of my life.
Today I feel hopeful -
    people, jobs, adventures,
    dinners with friends.
New energy will bounce off
    the walls of my cells,
    revitalizing my possibilities.
Life now is like living within the confines
    of the pinball machine on the pier -
    unplugged, no lights flashing,
    balls roll sluggishly forward -
    tentatively - no momentum - no spring.
Not enough push to go far -
    I have no interest in playing.
Even if I plug in the cord -
    electric current is intermittent.
I thought I felt hopeful - for a moment - still,
    I sit here pushing away the anxiety -
    the sense that my life is drifting -
    no purpose - no direction.
Trust that my soul is writing new chapters -
    unseen - written with invisible ink.
Stop worrying.
Hidden messages can be revealed with light.
Enlightenment - unlike the pin-ball machine
    which requires a connection with electricity and mechanics -
    is ignited with heightened awareness and trust.

Possibilities are calling me - I can feel them -
    eyes wide open float to the middle of the stream.
Relax and breathe deeply. Flow with the energy
    moving me to where I need to go.

Part III
BUILDING A COCOON
A Wiser Young Woman Rebuilds

A WALK ON THE BEACH IN AFRICAN HATS
A Different Kind of Intimacy

Who is this man - Paul Tracey?
Why do friends want us to meet?
I know he is a professional musician
    and storyteller.
He is from Durban, South African.
His wife died a year ago in a car crash.
He has two young children.
His father is a noted musicologist -
    who founded the International Library of African Music.

I was teaching at a conference at USC.
I arrived halfway through his lecture demo on
    African music, stories and culture.
I came in, crossed my legs and sat
    down on the floor with 100 others.

He stopped -
    looked straight at me and said,
        "Well, Hello!"
I was deeply embarrassed to be pointed out.
But - I was very late!

Afterwards, I went up to him and
    introduced myself.
Our mutual friend, Marianne Cummins,
    had suggested we meet.
He continued packing up his guitar, African instruments,
    gathered the hand of his little son
    and said, without looking at me,
"Well, if you'd like me to call,
    give your number to Marianne!"
He walked out of the room and
    left me standing there - watching!

Marianne already had my number -
    so I told her to tell him to call.
I was curious about this tall Englishman!
He left a message, saying,

"Well, I plucked up the courage to call.
If you have any courage, call me back!"

Shocked at his cheekiness -
    but also touched by his vulnerability,
    I returned his call.
We set a date for lunch at his house
    in Pacific Palisades.

On the set day and hour, I arrived
    and asked if I could take a shower.
I had just come from teaching
    a dance class.
I was sweaty - it was summer!
He was somewhat shocked -
    but led me to a shower.
Refreshed, I met him in his kitchen.
He had a long loaf of French bread,
    cheeses and a bottle of wine.
I interviewed him about his life.
He was unique, shy, humorous and
    fascinating.

He asked if I would like to join him in a
    walk on the beach - nearby.
I said, *"Yes!"*
He left for a moment
    then returned with two extraordinary
    African hats for us to wear!
He handed them to me and said,
    "Take your pick!"
I was rather horrified!
Did he actually want us to
    walk on the beach in these
    handmade LeSotho curiosities?

But, I wasn't going to show my shock.
I picked the smaller of the two
    and we climbed into his car.

Parking in front of the waves,
    we ventured out, side by side,
    our hats low on our brows,
    shielding our eyes. He is 6'3 and I am 5'4 -
Barefooted, there was a big gap in height.
We were quiet -

Then, he began to talk -
    with eyes straight ahead,
    he opened up about his English/African background,
    his parent's divorce, boarding the Capetown Castle with Ursula -
    his mother - and Andrew - his brother, and
    waving good-bye to his father as they sailed to England,
    not knowing seven years would pass
    before they would meet again!

He told me about his stage show, "Wait a Minim!"
    which started in Johannesburg, going to Broadway
    and eventually touring the world for seven years.
He spoke lovingly of his wife, Barbara Quaney,
    who auditioned in New York and
    got the role because he had the final vote!
They married, while on tour in San Francisco.
He told me about his children, Sarah and Devon.

He told me about his work with the
    American Wind Symphony Orchestra
    traveling the rivers of America -
    writing original songs for each port.
He told me how he tragically lost his wife
    and how a former nanny for Sarah - the wonderful Belinda -
    had flown in from Australia
    and stayed for months to rescue him.

There was more - I listened . . .
My heart grew soft and opened to him -
    his story.
We continued to walk in a straight line
    never looking directly at each other.
When we reached Gladstones, we turned around
    and headed back.

His story continued to present time,
    being a single dad,
    bringing in a former nannie,
    Belinda, from Australia, to help.
His best friend, Jamil, flying in from New York
    to assist in raising his children.
His work performing in schools.
He was busy, but still a light-hearted man
    with a large load to carry on his back.
He finished . . . I asked questions . . .
We got in the car and
    drove back to his home.

He took me into his garden,
    picked a small bouquet of his zinnias for me
    along with three Gem squashes he'd grown -
    perfectly round -
    one for me, Julie and Heather.

This was a walk to remember - the two
    African Hats now hang on our wall!

A HONEYMOON IN SCOTLAND

Heather,
Like spoonfuls of
Raspberry Jam
Squeezed from giant
Tarts
Dripping down the
Chins
Of gargantuan mountain
Men
Titillating my taste
Buds
To picnic in their
Laps -
My mouth open
Wide.
My senses are alive!

COMBINING GROUPS

Power struggles
To gain territorial rights
In each other's universe.
Gerrymandering.

THE TUILERIES GARDENS – PARIS

Rainbow boats
Of patchwork cloth
Sail with my fantasies
On a fountained pool
In Paris
Through a shimmering afternoon.

Prismed water,
Chiseled crystals of light
Reflected in the
Eyes of my children
As they send their boats forth on a ripple.

Devon, Sarah and Heather - three sailors
Each with a long stick and a dream.
Ride your boat -
Let it carry your
Imagination as far as
It will go.

MY DEEPEST LOSS

When my daughter Julie was killed
    in a car crash at 19,
    I thought I had tumbled off
    the edge of the world.
Not only did she shape me as a mother,
    but expanded my heart -
    to feel joy, solve problems,
    love, play and find my best self.
I couldn't forget my other daughter -
    Heather -
    a beautiful soul.
Both she and I would lose so much more if
    we couldn't recover.
It was a journey of crawling
    along the ground together,
    noses pushed into the dirt.

Resting for many years in a
    safe cocoon of quiet growth,
    we both emerged as healed people,
    mostly free of fear, loss and anger.
I have survived through
    the love of friends and family.
Heather has survived because she found
    the courage to live her life fully.
I admire her so much for that,
    for her grace, kindness and sense of humor.
My forever love is dedicated to
    Heather and Julianne.

JULIANNE

Julianne
You are gone.
I am broken.
I have no words.
Only tears, tears and more tears
raining from within.
I am drowning in rivers of loss.
I search for you - but cannot find you.
Yet, you still live in my heart.

OFF WITH MY BREAST!

My diagnosis - breast cancer.
The remedy - off with my breast!
Don't tell!
Don't tell my ex-husband.
I even ask our daughter not to tell him.

He will think I brought it on myself.
Judgment! Advice! Admonishment!
My own fault!
"Earth to Susan,
　　Earth to Susan!"
His way of getting my attention.
Shooting an arrow into my daydreams -
　　shattering my thoughts,
　　　jerking me back into reality.

Well, I am standing
　　right now in stark reality.
Life has seldom felt
　　more painful.
I am scared.
I am ashamed.

I want to go to bed
　　deep under my covers.
No! Don't tell my ex-husband!

The phone rings.
My husband Paul answers.
He says, *"Oh, Hi Lee!"*
It's my ex-husband!
"How's Susan?"
"Interesting you should ask.
She has cancer - breast cancer.
Yes, just diagnosed,
    she's scared!
The operation is
    the day after Christmas.
I'll tell her you called.
I'm sure she would like to talk.
Give her a call!"

Under my covers
    I hear my worst secret being told
    by my loving husband
    to my ex-husband!
Shame, fear and anger
    rise up within me!

MY ATTITUDE NOW

Fortunately,
    I didn't have to make a decision about chemicals or radiation.
I am one of the lucky ones.
Cancer is a crap shoot -
    no one knows if Lady Luck will sit atop their shoulder
    or completely abandon them.
Lady Luck was on my shoulder,
    whispering advice quietly into my ear - my doctor's ear.
Luck can abandon us in an instant!

I acted swiftly,
    learning that it takes only one rogue cancer cell
    to start colonies in our organs.
They quickly claim the territory,
    reconfiguring our landscape,
    setting up hostile villages,
    challenging our warrior cells to join in warfare -
    for our lives.

I was saved from chemo and radiation by my cells
    building calcium castle walls to enclose the enemy.
Unlike chemical soldiers,
    my warrior cells could not conquer and kill.

Rather,
    they held these cancer gangs prisoner
    within my home-made barriers -
    until the surgical team could remove them
    from my battleground!

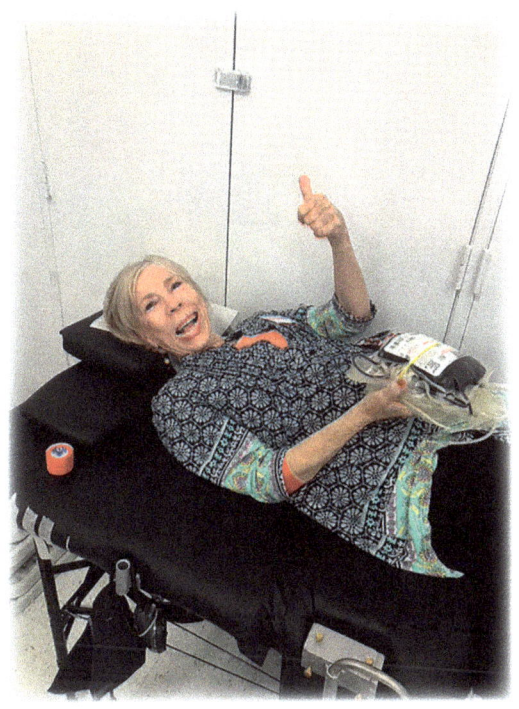

FIRST SAVE YOURSELF

Can anyone save the world?
Can anyone save themselves?
Can anyone save another?
Should they?
What is a truly selfless act?
What is an act of courage?
Heroes don't see themselves as courageous,
    they do what is required –
    without thinking of themselves.
Angels don't see themselves as special,
    they are kind and caring,
        they act compassionately when they see a need, a pain,
    or a challenge.

They give all that is required
    without thought of reward or self.

What is a truly selfless act?
What is an act of courage?
Acting swiftly, without thought of consequences,
    righting a wrong in a moment in time.

When you give and deplete yourself,
    is this healthy?
When someone demands your fealty without question or thought,
    is this morally right?
Some people become slaves,
    no matter their gender, skin color, ethnicity or age,
    falling under the spell of power and might.
Some people expect others to follow them without question -
    dictators, crime family dons, professors,
    doctors, police, some parents and spouses.

There is a difference between compassion and control.
When being controlled or controlling others,
    one abdicates responsibility to stay true
    to one's moral code.
They give their power away.
Compassion is a sympathetic awareness of others' distress
    and a desire to alleviate it.
Personal responsibility and good choices are empowering.

My father was a combination of control and compassion.
However, at the end of every situation,
    compassion would win out.

Part IV

A BUTTERFLY EMERGES & TAKES FLIGHT

A Changed Woman Finds Her Power

RED-TAILED HAWK - FREEDOM THROUGH PERSPECTIVE

Freedom!
A new perspective.
A body built for flight.
Wings decorated with overlapping rows
    of luminous brown feathers,
        shimmering as sunlight reflects.

Feet,
    with claws to kill –
    clasp - carry -
    balance on rocks, ledges and branches -
    free to perch -
    free to explore.

Eyes to see things others miss.
Power to fly, dive and soar.
Catching rides on currents of air.
Freeways in the skyway.

Dive into valley floors.
Soar to rocky cliffs.
Nesting into high, hidden rocks.
Space is my canvas.

My wings, the tips of brushes
    painting with rainbow breath.
Power lives in my wings.

Legs tucked up into my soft feathers,
    like wheels of a plane,
        hidden in the belly of the craft.

When I do Sun Salutations,
    I am this bird,
    my human body gets a chance to fly.
As my chest lifts
    my arms spread like graceful wings.
This ritual reminds me that
    my Spirit is free.

I just need to remember that
    I know how to fly.

NO FUNNY BONE

I'm missing a funny bone.
I laugh at life - not at jokes.
Humor can be cruel -
    funny for some - not for all -
    especially the one being mocked.
Sometimes humor is silly -
    not for me.
A few jokes are funny.
I laugh.
Many are not.
I am polite.

My husband Paul is light-hearted.
His emotional skeleton
    is composed of funny bones.
He lightens any conversation -
    sometimes ones that are serious.

I think he found me a challenge.
He stayed interested
    to make me laugh.
He got hooked.
Sometimes he makes me smile -
    that makes him smile.

He finds jokes just for me -
    saves them -
    emails them to me.
I like the gesture more than the jokes!
Sometimes he hits the bulls-eye!
I laugh out loud -
    he is happy!

His intention is to
    make me less serious about life.
Mine is to make him more serious.
Together, we have achieved
    a delicate balance!

WHAT CAN I CHANGE - WHAT CAN I NOT?

At about age 40,
    I began to see signs of aging.
Until then,
    I liked the changes I saw.
I became more developed,
    grew into my potential.
My skin had a glow after motherhood.
Then…

in my early 50s,
> the beginning signs of Menopause appeared -
> skin wrinkled,
> weight mysteriously increased,
> muscles became less firm,
> strands of gray appeared in my hair,
> eyebrows thinned,
> my one remaining breast began to droop,
> my well aligned teeth begin to shift -
> crossing over into each others' spaces!

So, I dyed my hair,
> changed to a low fat diet,
> got expensive makeup,
> increased my workouts,
> got my nails done bi-weekly.

Things looked better -
> although not the same.

More acceptable - not ideal,
> different hair-cuts,
> new fashions - looser -
> Yoga - to calm my fears.

My daughters,
> growing more beautiful as they grew older,
> I,
> looking more and more like a middle-aged woman -
> no longer getting compliments from men -
> just long-time women friends.

Then…

I turned 60!
I had less parenting stress in my life.
My adult children took on their own issues.
My work was challenging and fulfilling.
My marriage was happy -
    and, still is!
I decided to accept myself -
    my aging process.

An attitude changed deep within,
    spiritual work rather than physical makeovers,
    reality rather than illusions.
My style -
    unique and creative.
My hair -
    woven to include the gray.
My weight -
    back to the weight of my youth.
More veggies –
    although I am not a fan.
Fewer burritos and Margaritas,
    more salads, lighter desserts -
    still ... a glass of red wine with dinner.
Now...

At 80,
    the make-over is within.
Acceptance for who I am -
    for what I survived.
I accept that life is only a bleep in time.
Even though I believe our souls are on a continuum,
    I will never again have the life I have now.
I see it as an evolving work of art -
    and...
Love what is emerging from years of living it.

GIVE, TAKE, HOLD ONTO - OR LET GO

I like my life -
    honest, trusting, playful, fluid.
I have completed my main jobs.
I found and married my true love -
    we trust and respect each other.

Our children have their own lives.
I have planted many seeds,
    pulled acres of weeds,
    rebuilt relationships
    or released them.

I have survived jealousy,
    loss, sadness, fear,
    anger and physical pain.
I feel balanced.
I feel hopeful.
I have accepted myself,
    celebrated my accomplishments,
    forgiven my adversaries,
    forgiven myself.

I realize that
    change is the only constant.
Life is a series of
    Beginnings and Endings.

I am kind, trustworthy, loving -
    and -
    can also set boundaries
    so others do not intrude
    or take advantage of me.

I am working to fulfill every moment.
When it is time, I hope to turn
    into fine, white ashes,
        gently scattered by the wind.

AN ARCHEOLOGICAL DIG THROUGH PHOTOS

Seven and a half months of alone time -
    more than I've had
    in seven and a half years!
I feel like a hamster
    running quickly on her wheel -
    staying in the same place.

All the things on my check list
    - except cleaning -
    are checked off - in red ink!
Sooooooo,
    I embarked on an archaeological dig
    into my life - this life -
    which seems like a few thousand years ago -
    finding relics from my past.

Time to read journals written decades ago,
    the same issues revisited
    over many years now.
Boxes of faded photos - some surprising -
    some familiar - some seen with new eyes.
How many photos do I need? Want?
Feel obligated to keep?
Memories creep into my mind.
I play out the melodies of my life
    on an emotional accordion.

Images of myself in recent,
    but seemingly ancient times.
Years have passed,
    yet people remain the same in photos.
Some who appear before me are dead.
Smiling at the camera
    they are alive in my heart.

I see my two daughters,
    a few days old - yet four years apart.
I see each of my grandchildren -
    soon after their births.
I see myself as a baby,
    in my mother's arms.
We could all be toddlers together.
Different settings - different times.

Next, we are all teens -
    only our clothing and settings
    betray the truth.
Different eras - different styles.

In my personal digging,
    I see all of my family as young,
    dreams shining in our eyes.
All on a quest -
    different adventures
    made possible - or necessary
    by different events,
    political systems and inventions.
Being alone for longer than I wanted
    has given me a gift.
I dig up and examine
    the treasures and lessons.
Challenges given to my generation became
    opportunities, disappointments and encounters.

COVID-19 is a bleep in time -
    enforced alone time
    was seen by me
    as restrictive punishment -
    something to endure.

In writing this poem, I realize
    Extra Alone Time is a gift -
    I am finally unwrapping it.

A RITE OF PASSAGE FOR SKYLAR

Summer of 2021.
Skylar is my grand-daughter,
    she is 13.
She visits every summer.
This summer she wants to get
    her ears pierced -
    a rite of passage -
    from childhood to teens.

Her mother is against this.
However, she made a deal -
    if Skylar gets up on time . . .
    if she is cooperative . . .
    if she shows a positive attitude
    throughout their vacation -
    she can get them pierced
    on the last day!
Susu (me) can take her to
    get this dastardly deed done!

Days pass . . . weeks pass . . .
I teach Skylar to make pierced earrings.
I keep them safe for her -
    she longs to wear them!
Then, their vacation is almost over -
    two days to go.
Skylar has passed the test -
    she gets permission -

I go into action -
> make an appointment at
> CVS Beauty Counter -
> this is the first time they are piercing ears -
> probably to sell earrings!

CVS seems mild and sanitary -
> earring guns create the holes.

Ouch! - but, quick.
We get up early the next day -
> our appointment is at 9:30 a.m.

We show up - the woman is not there!
She called in sick!
We are devastated -
> it has to be today -
> or wait another year!

We return to the car.
We both get on our cell phones
> calling places that pierce ears.

No one answers -
> no answering machines!

Aren't they open?
We'll never know.

Skylar is good at phone research!
She finds tattoo parlors -
> body piercing.

Most at Venice Beach -
> no one answers.

We decide to drive there -
> walk until we find a place open.

How dangerous can a tattoo parlor be?
Do they use adequate antiseptics?
Are they board-certified?
They DO have experience - unlike CVS!

It is now 10:30 a.m.
I must be back to teach yoga at noon.
Can we do this?
We both give it our best!
Skylar uses her phone map to
    find each place on her list.
None are open!

We walk up and down the boardwalk -
    then, we see a man put out
    a sandwich-board sign -
"BuzzBomb Tattoos and Body Piercings"
Welcome!
A gust of excitement -
    we rush inside.
A very large, bearded,
    tattooed man - many body piercings -
    standing there.
He is - at first glance - scary!
He's nice.

I said we want
    Skylar's ears pierced -
    her rite of passage!
Can he do this?
YES!
A master piercer!

Her great desire fueling her courage,
>   bravely she sits down.
Like a knight, he prepares himself
>   for this deed.
She sits there -
>   eyes forward.
Then, the deed is done!
She has officially completed her
>   Rite of Passage.

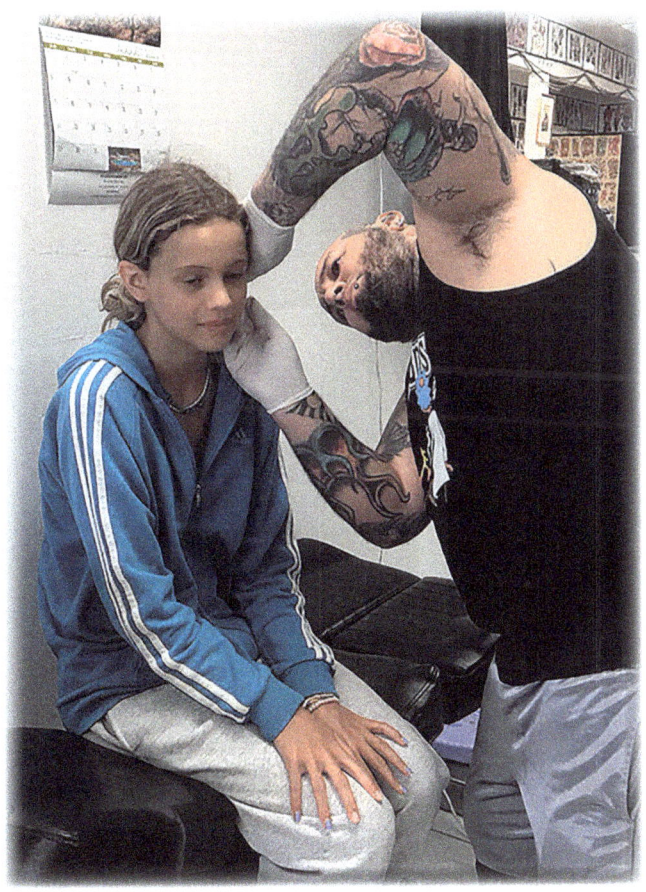

A VIRTUAL BUCKET LIST

Dreams are like air.
A sky filled with clouds -
    different shapes
    depending on weather conditions -
    wispy - foreboding - big puffs of whipped cream.
Sometimes the skies are empty,
    blue skies - grey skies - evolving colors.
Dreams, like a breeze,
    rustling leaves on trees,
    but no visions,
    no urges,
    just space.

So far, I have fulfilled many things
    on my bucket list.
Children,
    happy marriage,
    purpose for my life.
Work allowing me to support that purpose.
Loving, wise and generous friendships,
    enough money,
    material things,
    a good and comfortable life,
    healthy food - a home - a car - clothes of my choosing -
    comfortable shoes to walk in,
    earrings,
    a healthy body.

 Unexpected adventures
    in both common and uncommon places -
      Alaska - Maine - Arizona - New Orleans -
      Oregon - Missouri - Vermont - North Carolina -
      Minnesota - Hawaii - Tennessee - Puerto Rico -
      England - France - Germany - Mexico - Thailand - Korea -

    South Africa - Zimbabwe -
    Egypt - Spain - Greece - Turkey.
Interactions with different cultures and personalities.
Meeting kind and caring strangers.

What's left?
To become a high flyer - a Trapeze acrobat -
    dance with Jiri Kilian -
Have him choreograph
    a piece for me
    inspired by an animal
    embodying my personality -
    perhaps from the cat family -
    an independent spirit,
    a bit wild, yet loves soft blankets,
    lying in the sun, stretchy poses,
    and having its back rubbed.

Maybe a red-tailed Hawk.
I do like to fly - but get queasy
    on a ladder - a rooftop,
    and looking down
    into the Grand Canyon.

Yet, I want to fly!
Be free - soar and dive -
    ride the air currents in a cloudless sky.
Rise above the sun-sets.
Leap off high cliffs in a flying suit.

I did fly in a parachute pulled by a boat
    in Cancun, Mexico.
Was carried by a balloon in
    Cappadocia, Turkey.
But now -
    I am at an age where I might
    decide to complete my bucket list …
Virtually!

PASSAGES - RITES OR RIGHTS?

Celebrate a passage in my life.
Challenges - Struggles - Engagement - Change.
Finally, a time when the task is done,
    the journey completed,
        all requirements met.

There is fear in completing something.
What comes next?
Routines are geared to support a goal -
    structure and discipline required for success.
Once a big goal is reached -
    fear of nothingness -
    I stand in uncluttered space.

Now...
The Pandemic is beginning a new phase.
I can drop my safe routines -
    staying at home close to my base.
Resume trips to work and back.
Visits with friends.
Big adventures.
How do I transition
    between home alone
    and the world beyond home?
Take more risks again?

Is it safe?
Comfortable in my own kingdom -
    home, garden, personal office and studio.
Do I want to venture beyond the block?
A new mentality -
    goings and comings
    rather than the comfort
    of my personal space.

My inner world has evolved.
The outer world has diminished.
Can I go out into the world again -
    without losing all I have gained going within?

THE MOVIE VERSION OF MY LIFE

The movie version of my life is animated. . .
Watercolor drawings -
    showing life in a magic forest -
    whispering trees sharing ancient secrets -
    flying squirrels carrying messages from tree to tree,
    circulating the story of my life - in different forms.

Haven't I been on this quest before?
Haven't I been searching for truth through eternity?
Haven't I asked for guidance?
Haven't I given my best efforts to moving my story -
    our story - forward?
Like fairy tales caught in the confines of the original script,
    I feel stuck
        reliving life after life in the same pursuit.

Who am I?
Where am I actually from?
What am I supposed to do
    now that I'm here?
Who am I supposed to work with?
Why?
What is it all about?
We are alone, but together.
We are together, but still alone.

Why did COVID-19 descend upon us?
What does it have to teach?
Is it happenstance - or a critical part of our human journey?
All for one or one for all?
Alone or together?
Masks to make us safe?
Or. . .
Masks to confine our freedom?

I digress - back to the movie of my life, or lives.
Where does it go from here?
Whispering trees telling this ancient,
    repetitive story with variations.
Flying squirrels with updates!
Shy deer witnessing the story unfold,
    telling no one.
Sly snakes winding their way through the tall meadow grasses,
    slithering along branches for a meal
        of vulnerable eggs lovingly tucked into nests.

Who has the questions? Who has the answers?
Who has the storyteller's pen?
Is my story just a modernized variation of the original?
Can I break free of my archetype?
Am I stuck reliving the same story - different costumes - different times?

What if I'm tired of my costume? What if I have outgrown it?
It is now too small to fit my expanded self.
Perhaps I no longer need a costume
    or a character to dramatize.
What if I've outgrown the storybook versions of myself?
What then?
No costumes to wear . . . no memorized lines to speak . . .
No limited view of my environment . . .
Friends released to be themselves,
    rather than play their part in my life?

The freedom to change,
    do things differently,
    be myself without fitting a prototype - a gender - a race - an age.
True freedom!

Is COVID-19 here to force evolution -
    like the great flood, wiping out most of humanity?
Saving a group to transform
    into more compassionate and inclusive beings?
One for all - all for one?
I wonder . . . as I wait to complete this life's movie version
    of my continuing journey . . .

Part V
FREE FLIGHT – SOARING
A Mature Woman Accepts Death, Claiming her Life Force

AN IDEAL RELATIONSHIP

What I now want from a relationship
    is different from what
    I wanted when I was younger.
I have grown to value
    Trust
    Honesty
    Love and Friendship
    Laughter - not at one - but with one
    Acceptance
    Generosity
    Common interests,
    Thoughtful Conversations about Life

A balanced emotional relationship is stronger
    than physical attraction and sex.
Kindness is more important
    than appearance.
Laughter is more important
    than money.
Friendship is more important
    than prestige and power.
Acceptance is more important
    than pride -
The need to be right
    destroys relationships.

Going to bed together -
    touching feet in the dark.
The calm and even breathing
    of peace and trust.
Waking up together -
    realizing you're both alive and well.
Greeting the day together
    with possibilities
    rather than complaints.

Feeling the many blessings of
    sharing life with the one you love -
    and who loves you.
Having common goals,
    as well as separate ones.
Conflicts resolved with respect and fairness.
Forgiving yourself so that you can
    forgive your partner.
Grudges released - broken down into compost -
    the past re-edited to build a future.

JOY IN BED

Lying in bed next to my husband,
    I feel peaceful, happy, fulfilled and safe.
At night we cuddle - or - if too tired,
    just touch feet.
If it's cold,
    I put my feet on his thighs to get warm -
    he endures it.
In the morning,
    I feel joy in knowing he is there beside me -
    wearing a black eye mask
    because I stay up watching TV.
I awake and am amazed that we are both alive
    and have another day to unwrap together.
We wake up in stages,
    then share our dreams.
We check our emails -
    sharing with each other.
We laugh,
    we snuggle,
    we share our plans for the day -
    knowing as we age -
    our time together shortens.
We bask in the cozy intimacy
    of being together in bed.

CHANNEL A TREE

Tall or short, thin or wide -
    we all have roots
    deep into the earth,
    branches broad, strong and flexible.
When winds blow - violent instability -
    trees hold steady -
    trunks bending - leaves shuddering -
    branches crack - some fall,
    yet most trees hold firm.

People blow past me -
    nothing to cling to, no deep roots -
    not even a thought to keep them balanced.
Challenged to my core,
    I strive for balance -
    righting myself as bad weather looms.

Holding my space
    I am strong, flexible, rooted -
    even as leaves are shaken from my branches
    and I stand bare and exposed - shivering,
    my trunk sways, my roots cling to unstable earth -
    but I hold my ground - and breathe.

Inhale . . . Exhale
Inhale courage - Exhale fear
Inhale hope - Exhale despair
Inhale confidence - Exhale doubt
Inhale determination - Exhale excuses
Inhale . . . Exhale
I breathe - I am alive.

As a tree, I inhale what people exhale,
    CO_2 photosynthesizes into O_2.
My inhales take in emotional toxins -
    but, I transform negativity into possibilities.

Standing strong and flexible,
    I stay balanced -
    holding space for those needing
    protection, courage and perspective.
Climb into my branches; rest awhile.
A safe haven awaits you -
    rest awhile.
Don't be afraid. You are safe.
Hold on - look upon the landscape.
There is a sunrise after this moment.
You can then climb down . . .
    refreshed.

IF I COULD CHOOSE -
I WOULD WANT A GARDENER

I grew up in a family who created a field of love -
    then planted me and my brother in the soil.
They applied the knowledge
    learned when they were planted,
    nourished and raised by their parents.
Both grew up in the early 20th Century.
Their families were intelligent, courageous, and poor.

Still, they worked hard,
    took responsibilities early in life,
    learned that children grow best when they are encouraged.

They were rooted in a potting mixture of hard work,
    discipline and kindness.
Everyone contributed to the survival of the family.

Because of things my parents learned from their parents,
    I know what it feels like to belong to a kind family -
    to be loved and valued.
I learned about Honor,
    Respect, Responsibility, Commitment, and Cooperation.
Doing things when I didn't want to -
    Facing all problems with courage.

Both my parents loved to garden, cook,
    and have intelligent conversation during family dinners.
My Dad was a judge,
    so we were often given court cases to discuss.
Each was asked to take one side and defend it.

His mentors were Abraham Lincoln
    and the American writer, Horatio Alger Jr. *
We learned the importance of truth and justice for all.
No one was above, or below, the law.
Eventually justice would prevail.

Life wasn't always fair.
The laws would protect all of us!
We were encouraged to think,
    find ways to contribute,
        to be Kind, Truthful, Fair -
        Work hard!

All of this nurturing by my parents
    shaped who I have become.
These are the same tools I have used
    to help my children and grandchildren grow,
        seeing that each is different,
        each is unique -
        each is valued.

So, in this COVID-19 Pandemic -
    sequestered at home -
    with one person
    I realize that he needs to be a Gardener.
Someone who brings the sun into my days,
    a smile, kind acts, and loving touch,
    a man who finds wonder in the natural world,
    who respects all the plants growing in his personal garden.
A man who knows that we are unique seeds -
    planted, nourished,
    encouraged to bud, blossom,
    AND
    eventually wither and die.

My ideal partner in this precious, yet isolating time,
    is Paul Hugh Lawrence Tracey -
    my husband - Gardener and Musician.
He hears the songs of nature -
    realizes we are all part of the music.
He loves and appreciates beauty.
I am so happy that I have this timeless opportunity
    to spend in awe and gratitude -
        being appreciated, cared for, and loved.

---

* Horatio Alger was an American writer of young adult novels about impoverished boys and their rise from humble backgrounds to lives of middle class security and comfort through hard work, determination, courage, and honesty.

MY COVID BUBBLE

It is October, 2020.
We are in the COVID-19 Pandemic!

This is when it counts.
This is when I am reaping the benefits
    of choosing a playful partner.
He actually said early on that I have made him
    more serious about life.
If that is true,
    then, he has made me
    more light-hearted.

Yes,
    I still aspire to set challenging goals,
    bold and rigid deadlines.
But, I have more fun in the process!

My life partner takes my hand
    and leads me out to his garden -
There are miracles happening
    here in the dirt.

He shows me humming birds and bees,
    even a snake!
He points out the yellow butterflies
    flitting around the Golden Wonder tree.
He transports me into a world
    that he designed -
Full of beauty, wonder, change and
    a large family of lizards.

He picks bouquets of flowers
    from his garden - grown from seed,
    places them in a Hint water bottle
    at the bottom of the staircase.
I feel special as I descend the stairs.

I enter his office, and he shows me jokes!
He takes pleasure in making me laugh.
We sit across from each other at meals
    taking turns reading "Dear Amy" letters.
We take time to hear people's problems,
    then sincerely try to think what
    advice we would give them,
    guiding their choices
    to create a happy life -
    like we have.

My husband finds humor in
    just about everything -
But,
    does not make fun
    of people or their situations.
He is like a tall Garden Gnome who shyly smiles at you,
    from under his hat,
    letting you know that whatever happens,
    he will do his best to support you.

He is strong of character,
    but doesn't impose his will on others.
He cries when something touches his heart.
He plays games of all types to keep his mind alert.
I don't like playing games,
    but I do like playing house with Paul.

A FAIRY TALE THAT NEEDS A HAPPY ENDING

Once Upon a Time
    we were living our lives
Alone and Together,
    here, there and everywhere.

Collectively we evolved, although . . .
    each individual had a unique story to live and tell -
    perhaps evolving, but maybe not.

But then,
    an unplanned journey -
    a nightmare with no escape
    came to Our Global World.
A grotesque fairy tale enveloped us.

All the archetypes are present -
    villains, heroes, innocents, opportunists,
The Brave - cowards - wise ones - fools,
    Self-righteous, Self-centered and Arrogant,
    selfless, courageous and unafraid.
They're all appearing in this tale!
All the roles are cast.
Everyone is included!

Most are compassionate and kind -
    some are detached - a few are cruel.

How do we wind our way through this dark mystery
    into the light
Alone . . . and, yet together?
We do it alone and together!

How do we keep writing our individual stories
    in the middle of a bigger one?
Recognize that the collection of smaller stories creates the bigger tale!

How do we plant the seeds of hope in ALL minds?
We need fertile soil and care

How do we nourish each person?
With love, compassion, trust and strength

What about the self-righteous,
    those stuck in denial, grief, fear and rage?
These are all part of the human palate of emotions -
First, truly listen.
Speak with kindness and understanding

Everyone is needed to determine the ending of this tale.
Scientists, leaders, medical professionals, essential workers,
    insiders and outsiders, teachers, parents, elders,
    neighbors and the disenfranchised.
ALL the members of our Global Tribe are needed!

ALL have a voice in the writing of this story.
No one is left out. . . ALL are included.

As an Elder in our Global Community
>   I ask for Seven Blessings
>   to guide us
>   as we write, and act our way
>   through this mystery:

1
Unity and fellowship
>   *as we work together*

2
Compassion, Kindness and Support,
>   *given freely with universal love*

3
Seeing ourselves in others,
>   *seeing others in ourselves*

4
Hope and Possibilities
>   *rather than Loss and Fear*

5
Responsible thoughts and actions
>   *by everyone*

6
Egos released
>   *avoid Blaming and Shaming*

7
Solve problems with wisdom and haste

ALONE TIME - TOO MUCH?

Alone time is good for my soul.
I had a lot of alone time when I was growing up.
This helped me develop interests and hobbies.
Then, as a student, teacher, mother and wife,
    I had almost no alone time.
I craved alone time -
    to feel who I am without the energy of others
    bouncing in, out, and around me -
    at times binding me.

There was never enough
    Alone Time.
My time belonged to my work, to dance,
    to my husband, children, parents and friends.

Then . . . my work declined.
My parents died.
I divorced my first husband -
    the father of my children.
As a single mom -
    I had even less time alone.
Years passed . . .
I remarried, embracing two more children.

There was absolutely no time for myself.
Shopping, cleaning, preparing meals,
    going to games and concerts, homework, family trips.
Year by year, my children grew up,
    appropriately, they left our little home,
    seeking adventures and
    starting families of their own.

I retired from one career -
    embraced another,
    which required more training, more teaching,
    and more marketing.
We became grandparents -
    all of our children living long airplane rides away.
My free time became weddings, births,
    travel time, grandmother time,
    a whirl of new activities,
    concerts and school performances.

I thought I just loved being active -
    no down time for me -
    unless it was recovering from an injury -
    there were a few.
Unplanned time is a waste.
I continued to have a rigorous schedule of teaching,
    coaching, administrating,
    designing and implementing workshops,
    Yoga, Pilates, being with friends.
We built a yoga studio.
 I scheduled more classes.

During my marriage, Paul invited me
    into his garden,
    to share afternoon tea,
    luring me to listen as he played his guitar and sang.
I interrupted my schedule to accept these gifts -
    even if there wasn't time.
I carved it out of my busy schedule.

THEN
>   seven months ago, the COVID-19 Pandemic hit -
>   one week after a series of four parties
>   to celebrate my 80th Birthday.

My birthday season was the entire month of February!
My daughter came to visit for a week -

THEN - BOOM!
Lockdown!! Schools canceled, businesses closed.
Our world changed to
>   Zoom meetings and Masks!!!

We were told to stay at home -
>   no teaching, or taking yoga classes.

No more driving to work -
>   we now work from home!

No need for beauty treatments.

WE CAN ALL GET SICK!
SOME MAY DIE!
WHAT A SHOCK!
WHAT A CHANGE!!

Now I have time alone.
Time to enjoy things without a schedule.
At first I tolerated it!
I felt like a racehorse at the starting gate -
>   full of tension ready to burst forth at the sound of a gun!

I couldn't relax into nothingness.
I kept myself mentally and physically prepared
>   to spring into action.

I was wired for action -
>   not for stillness and quiet.

I didn't want to be alone!

NOW

I am learning to enjoy taking time to
    breathe more fully -
    not as yoga practice
    but anytime during the day.
I stop and consciously breathe.

I enjoy my husband's garden - at unscheduled times,
    sit down and slowly sip a cup of Turmeric tea.
My brain has enjoyed the break,
    allowing me to
    create outside a timeline.
Time has stretched out -
    but feels more fleeting.
And, rather than being bored,
    I have become more curious and lighthearted.
Off the grid.
Time Alone is now well spent!

EMPTY SPACES, TURTLES AND TIME

My life -
    a patchwork quilt
    sewn together with threads of energy and time.
Empty time seems boring -
    colors of grey, white, black and brown.
Fulfilled time is exciting, full of bright colors
    of red, orange, yellow, green, purple and blue.

My quilt has memories sewn with love,
    joy, questions and pain.
It feels indulgent to squander time.
I don't want to waste
    a moment of my life.

I am reminded that music happens
    because of the spaces between the sounds.
Dance happens when
    movement and stillness are combined.
Energy is best when combined with rest.
Conversation works when one talks and one listens,
    when the speaker and listener change roles frequently.

I think of turtles on land - their slow pace
    combined with waiting and resting,
    houses carried on their backs.
They are always ready -
    slow and steady, also tedious.

Does a turtle get more,
    or less, out of living
    than a rabbit?
One is quick - one is slow.
One looks out and about -
    one scans the ground.

Does a turtle miss flying
    like a red-tailed hawk?
Does the hawk see more of the big picture?
Turtles see the ground in front of them,
    vaguely aware of the sky.
Do they wonder about flying?

The turtle moves slowly through time -
    does its life last longer?
The hawk moves with swift confidence -
    does it live a more fulfilling life?

Sea turtles are another matter.
In water they have grace and power -
    they can dive, swim and float.
They have a connection to water and land.

Do I want to live like a turtle,
    a rabbit or a red-tailed hawk?
Not a land turtle -
    perhaps a sea turtle,
    but definitely not a rabbit.
I like the free flight
    and space of a hawk's life.
Time is not spent in laborious travel,
    but in soaring, diving and exploring.
It's the Hawk's life for me -
    and, when I am finished,
    I want to explode
    into fiery feathers scattering -
    knowing I have fully lived!

THE GREATEST GIFT OF ALL

I have been starting to see each new day
    as possibly the last.
So, I seek to feel excited about
    the possibilities that present
    themselves each morning.
I wake up in the night sometimes
    and want to start the day early -
    I don't want to miss anything.
I start with a bath.
I begin with my toes and
    give gratitude for each and every body part.
Then I tell my husband
    how much I appreciate about him.
He fully accepts me for who I am.
Now,
    it is true that he doesn't fully understand me,
    nor does he always agree with me.
He accepts me anyway.
That is the greatest gift of all!

THERE . . . GO I

I saw a man in a wheelchair at the offramp
    of the freeway - begging for money.
We were stopped.
I had a chance to observe
    him carefully.
I could see that he felt shame at begging.
He felt less
    because he was in a wheelchair.
I got out a couple of dollars to give him,
    made the decision
    to really make eye contact with him,
    give him a sincere and loving smile,
    wish him well -
    with the belief that he could change his situation.
I rolled down my window.
Our eyes met.
I communicated friendship, belief and acceptance of him,
I wished him well -
    saying with my smile
    that I believed in him.
His sad and droopy face lit up
    like a chandelier with bright candles.
He smiled genuinely and broadly.
He got excited and spoke to my husband -

    "That is a truly beautiful woman."

There for the grace of God is me.
We must all see ourselves in each other.

A TRIP TO THE UNSEEN

The trip I most want to take
    is a trip to the place where
    souls go when they die -
    but without actually dying!
I would like to go with a guide
    who knows both worlds.

I don't want to get lost-
    stuck there
    with no way to return.

I just want to visit
>	long enough to greet
>	my daughter,
>	mother and father,
>	grand-parents
>	and a few friends.

Where are they now?
Can they still think - communicate - make plans?
Do they still have relationships?
Do they think of me?
Do they have jobs?
Are food and water needed?
Do they breathe?
Do they miss their bodies -
>	even if they were worn out,
>	diseased or broken?

Is their world filled with mountains, valleys, streams?
Is there weather?
How do they travel?
Do they think themselves into new places?
Is it boring? Is time a factor?
Are they living on spaceships or different planets?
Will I recognize them without bodies?
Will they recognize me?
Does love outlast death?

How much will this trip cost?
Can I pay with Karma Points?
What type of transportation will I need?
Can it happen in dreams?
Do I need a special outfit?

I do think I need a guide -
>   alive or dead -
>   who knows how to get there and back.

Can I trust him, her, they, them or it?

Is there an app
>   advertising such a trip -
>   making one possible?

Is it a place I've been before?
I'm ready -
>   just a bit apprehensive.

What shall I pack?

—EPILOGUE—

A VIEW FROM THE ROOF

Now,
in my early 80s,
I have climbed to the roof of my house.
I love the view from here.
It is exhilarating!
Paul and I sit here together on the ridge beside the chimney
knowing that at any instant one of us could fall.
But, as frightening as that is,
it is not unexpected.
We start alone - we end alone -
How fortunate we are to have found a compatible,
loving traveler with whom to share
our journeys and stories.

– BIOS –

SUSAN CAMBIGUE TRACEY'S BIO

Susan Cambigue Tracey is a dancer, arts administrator, nationally recognized educator, and a certified yoga instructor. She has written books and produced a documentary film about one of her many passions, namely, Chair Yoga. She graduated from UCLA with credentials in physical education/dance and became a dance therapist. Her legendary mentor, Bella Lewitsky, nominated Susan for a pioneering role with the National Artists-in-Schools Project. For fifteen years she traveled across the U.S. as a Dance Movement Specialist for the National Endowment for the Arts.

She founded and co-directed, with Slyvia Goulden, the Free Flight Improvisational Dance Company, performing in schools at the Brand Art Gallery in Glendale, CA for ten years, and in other aesthetic spaces, with their program called "Viewing Art through a Dancer's Eye."

 Susan has been on the dance faculty at Loyola Marymount University, and was Chair for the California Dance Educators Association as well as for the California Alliance for Arts Education. For 25 years, she held the position of Director of Curriculum and Teaching Artist Development for The Music Center of Los Angeles County, where she continues part-time.

Her life of words, in particular poetry, has caught up with her life in motion and the synergy has Susan creating hybrid pieces such as this book. She continues to refine her skills and sometimes redefine her life.

Although poetry and movement are her passions, her first loves are her husband, and often collaborator of 40 years, Paul Tracey, and an adored family of children and grandchildren living in America and Europe – all depicted in this book.

PAUL TRACEY'S BIO
in his own voice

Obviously, marrying Susan forty years ago was the smartest thing I have ever done in my life! But luckily I have had a few other moments, perhaps worthy of note. I was born in South Africa to a father of world renown for his work as an African musicologist. Raised in England with an accent that sounds as if I must be well educated, I farmed broiler chickens for a couple of years before breaking into show business almost by mistake. My brother and I created a stage musical revue called *Wait a Minim!* that began in Johannesburg and ran internationally for seven years, including 13 months on Broadway. This led to appearances on Johnny Carson's *Tonight Show*, and a classic bit on *Ed Sullivan's Show*. Marrying another cast member, we gave birth to two children who inspired me to become a song writer, and Jim Henson used four of my songs on *The Muppet Show* which the Disney Channel is kindly replaying this season. Abandoning my stage career because I don't speak American, I began my life as a wandering minstrel — a one-man-show man — creating 45-minute assembly programs mainly for elementary schools, on topics from African music and culture to the elements of good character that all children should acquire.

And then I love to garden. But when Susan calls, I run. To her — not away!

ACKNOWLEDGMENTS

I would like to acknowledge my parents, Martha and Ray Bennett, for being such strong and compassionate guides, inspiring me to become my best self. Without their guidance, I do not know that I would have the courage to not only survive some of the experiences that I lived through, but also the bravery to share these events with others. They practiced "tough love" that was extremely loving yet very strong.

I also want to thank Howard Kern, who really brought me back to my poetry by being so vulnerable in sharing his own writings and experiences with me. Additionally, I want to thank Barbara Ligeti for breathing life into the ShiftPoetry process and creating a safe and nurturing environment.

My utmost admiration and gratitude goes to my husband and life partner, Paul Tracey, for his complete acceptance of me for who I am, and his encouragement to be even more.

INDEX OF PHOTOGRAPHS

Section, Poem, and Page	Description	Year (circa)
Cover	Susan Cambigue Tracey ("Susan"), photo by Lee Hanson	1990
Dedication	Julianne Cambigue ("Julie")	1983
Preface	Susan	2013
Introduction	Susan	1990
Part I, Page 1	Susan with Mother Martha Bennett and Father F. Ray Bennett	1944
Jerry Gonzalez – My First Best Friend, Page 4	Susan and Jerry Gonzalez	1943
The Rag Doll, Page 7	Susan	1944
Reading to Find Meaning, Page 8	Susan and Student and Accompanist Mark Bucci	1976
Locked Up, Page 11	Susan's Father Judge F. Ray Bennett (Bampoo)	1991
She Is My Mother – But Not My Best Friend, Page 12	Susan with Mother	1944
My Last Meal, Page 17	Father and Paternal Grandfather Fred Bennett	1950
My Wise Guide, Page 20	Maternal Grandparents Rollo and Angie Rannells (Mambo and Dad Dad)	1954
Summers Past, Page 23	Susan	1945
Part II, Page 27	Susan	1957
A Perfect Birthday, Page 28	Susan, Husband ("Paul"), Daughter Sarah Tracey and Grandchildren Hugh and Skylar Tracey-Vickerman, artwork by Sarah Tracey	2018
Pets – A Source of Joy?, Page 29	Grandchildren Finn and Zach McKay and Pet Granddog Silver	2017
Trapeze Artist – A How-To Guide, Page 32	Julie, Susan's Daughter	1969
Death of a Princess, Page 41	Susan and Ex-Husband Lee Cambigue, photo by Alfred & Fabris	1962
The State of Abundance, Page 49	Susan and Red Mustang	1982
Part III, Page 55	Free Flight Improvisational Dance Company (Sylvia Goulden, Jo Ness, Susan, Lee Wasserwald, and Liz Oberstein)	1984
A Walk on the Beach in African Hats – A Different Kind of Intimacy, Page 56	Susan and Paul, photo by Lee Hanson	2000
A Honeymoon in Scotland, Page 61	Paul Tracey	1990
Combining Groups, Page 62	Susan with Children Sarah, Julie, Heather and Devon, photo by Frank Reuss	1982

Section, Poem, and Page	Description	Year (circa)
The Tuileries Gardens – Paris, Page 63	Paul and Susan, photo by Lee Hanson	1985
Julianne, Page 65	Julie	1968
First Save Yourself, Page 69	Susan	2021
Part IV, Page 73	Susan and Daughter Heather Cambigue McKay	2017
Red-Tailed Hawk - Freedom Through Perspective, Page 75	Susan and Musician Marilyn Sousa	1976
No Funny Bone, Page 76	Paul and Son Devon Tracey	2020
What Can I Change - What Can I Not?, Page 78	Susan	2019
Give, Take, Hold Onto - Or Let Go, Page 81	Grandson Hugh	2017
An Archeological Dig Through Photos, Page 83	Susan, Paul, and Granddaughter Bonnie Condron	2018
A Rite Of Passage For Skylar, Page 89	Granddaughter Skylar and Tattoo Artist	2021
The Movie Version Of My Life, Page 94	Susan and Friend Diana Cummins	2020
Part V, Page 99	Susan	2020
An Ideal Relationship, Page 100	Paul and Daughter Sarah	2018
Joy In Bed, Page 102	Paul	2018
Channel A Tree, Page 103	Son-In-Law Paul (Pablo) McKay and Grandson Finn	2007
If I Could Choose - I Would Want a Gardener, Page 105	Paul	2017
Empty Spaces, Turtles And Time, Page 117	Susan and Grandson Finn	2007
The Greatest Gift Of All, Page 120	Susan and Grandson Zach	2007
A Trip To The Unseen, Page 122	Paul and Grandson Finn	2013
Epilogue, Page 127	Susan	2021
Bios, Page 129	Susan and Paul	2018
Susan Cambigue Tracey Bio Page 130	Susan	2014
Paul Tracey Bio, Page 131	Paul & Young Paul (64 years apart)	2011, 1957
Back Cover	"Poem on White Shoes," Artwork and Photo - Heather McKay; Featured Poem - "First Save Yourself"	2020

www.ingramcontent.com/pod-product-compliance
Lightning Source LLC
Chambersburg PA
CBHW061208070526
44583CB00025B/3162